Sparks!

500 Writing Prompts to
Ignite Your Imagination

ELLEN MEISTER

For my students

CONTENTS

AUTHOR'S NOTE

One of the great pleasures of being an author has been the opportunity to teach creative writing to adults and young people. I love connecting with writers who understand the importance of studying their craft and improving their skills. (And for the record, that desire should never leave you. There is no "done" when it comes to studying writing.)

Part of this effort includes providing writing prompts that challenge and stimulate. For several years, I've been creating prompts specifically designed to help people take their writing skills to the next level, and I'm delighted to offer them here in his compilation.

This book is divided into five sections. Section 1, **General Prompts**, offers a miscellany of ideas to stimulate your imagination. Section 2 is **Themed Prompts**. These are presented almost as writing exercises. For example, one of the themes gives you the chance to choose from among five prompts to write about a person making a bad choice. Since effective fiction involves letting your characters behave badly and make mistakes, this exercise is designed to light that path. Section 3, **Advanced Themed Prompts**, offers the same kind of exercises with a bit more challenge. Section 4 lists **Opening Lines**, to help spark ideas. It can be astonishing to see how many different directions writers can take these prompts! The last section is **Word Prompts**, where you are given a set of five terms to use in a story. Since these are so popular, I've compiled all the word prompts from the first three sections into this unit, and added several more.

All the prompts are meant as jumping off points for your imagination, so feel free to use them in any way you choose. In other words, the answer to almost any question you can ask is *yes*.

Can I change the gender of the character?

Yes!

Can I choose a different setting?

Yes!

In the word prompts, can I change the tense of a verb?

Yes!

Can I combine two prompts?

Yes!

Take some time to familiarize yourself with the sections of this book ... or not. You can just dive in and figure it out as you go along. Be serious or silly. Be lyrical or minimal. Be wild or grounded. Be dark or light. Just keep writing. *Yes!*

SECTION 1
GENERAL PROMPTS

These 100 random prompts can be used however you wish. Skim the section to find your favorites, or pick a number and dive in!

1. After experiencing emotional trauma, your character loses the ability to understand sarcasm and irony. Everything is hyper-literal. What happens at a family dinner?

2. Write a story containing all of the following terms: *Ache, Fragile, Consent, Paper cup, Burden*

3. It's Thanksgiving, and your main character walks in on crutches. The story behind it is embarrassing, but she has no choice but to lay it all out for the group. Let the reader know who is in the room and why they're invested in the story.

4. An elementary school teacher has to keep his class of children calm during a lockdown in what is clearly a violent incident happening elsewhere in the building.

5. Write a story containing all of the following terms: *Introduced, Hovering, Devilled egg, Father, Sheepish*

6. Rewrite a multi-character scene from your work-in-progress, adding tension.

7. Think about the last time you had a fight or confrontation with a relative. Work it into a piece of fiction, changing pertinent details about the characters. Then let the characters drive the narrative.

8. During an anniversary dinner, the wife intentionally says some things to hurt the husband. Make sure the reader understands the pain that drives her actions.

9. Using your own emotions as your anchor, write about an adult experiencing the birth of a newborn. (Your character does not have to be the parent.) Make the *emotions* autobiographical, but not the story.

10. Write a story containing all of the following terms: *Lost, God, Bubbles, Gritted, Autistic*

11. Rewrite a scene from your work-in-progress, making the emotional story (but not the actual story) feel autobiographical to you.

12. Write a story containing all of the following terms: *Elevator, Clone, Whistle, Husband, Unlucky*

13. Your formerly overweight character has completely transformed their appearance. But

they cannot shed the internal issues that caused the obesity in the first place. Put them in a challenging scene.

14. Write a story containing all of the following terms: *Walled, Child, Backpack, Guilt, Necklace*

15. Rewrite a scene from your work-in-progress, but push your character into the position of making a moral choice.

16. Using an existing story (from TV, the movies or literature) as inspiration, write a scene as a fairytale.

17. Using a voice you wouldn't normally use, write a story containing all of the following terms: *Cigar, Beverly Hills, Fiery, Bartender, Alibi*

18. A teacher sees something disturbing in a child's drawing, and remembers an event from her own life.

19. When an elderly man learns his supermarket coupon has expired, he wonders if he should compromise his tight budget, or risk the embarrassment of admitting he no longer wants the item.

20. Write a story containing all of the following terms: *Impulse, Murmur, Diary, Billowy, Token*

21. Rewrite a story or a chapter from your work-in-progress, making a small incident loom large for your character.

22. To be or not to be? After a devastating accident that leaves your character physically handicapped, he or she wrestles with the idea of going on.

23. Your character's most cherished possession is destroyed (or stolen).

24. Write a story containing all of the following terms: *Vandalize, Unforgivable, Refrigerator, Persist, Morning*

25. Revisit a story or a chapter you had given up on.

26. Write an uncomfortable scene from the point of view of a high school bully who picks on a weaker kid. Go deep into the pain that drives the bully.

27. Write a story containing all of the following terms: *Martini, Aftershave, Charm, Sister, Testament*

28. A dying old person reveals a family secret … something that rocks your character to his or her core.

29. Write a story containing all of the following terms: *Hospital, Fracture, Sugary, Mother, Disney World*

30. Revise a chapter from your work-in-progress, incorporating feedback you have received from a reader, editor or fellow writer.

31. Your non-confrontational but highly principled character is torn up inside when dealing with someone making racist remarks. This can be a doctor/patient, employee/boss, family members or even strangers.

32. Your highly stressed character who feels entirely put-upon by the world is already in a state of road rage when hit in the rear at a traffic light. He exits, ready to unleash his fury, when he discovers the other driver is someone wrecked with grief from terrible news. Go

deep inside the protagonist's head to show us the shift in emotions.

33. Write a story containing all of the following terms: *frustrated, contagious, fog, Halleluiah, cologne*

34. Revise a chapter from your work-in-progress, giving the reader a deeper look into the character's emotional transition

35. Your character is just polishing off a bottle of wine when the doorbell rings. It's two police officers.

36. A teenager comes home at three am and knocks on their parents' bedroom door. "Mom?"

37. Think about the most selfish person you know. Create a character based on them, but imagine a scenario that inspires them to act selflessly.

38. Think about a time in your life that someone hurt you, and write a fictional scene about it ... but write it from the perspective of the other person.

39. Write a story containing all of the following terms: *Bitterness, Downtown, Paper bag, Miracle, Candle*

40. Revise a chapter from your work-in-progress, making it twenty percent shorter.

41. An adult woman is disillusioned to discover that the father she worshipped has been cheating on her mother for years.

42. Your character has recently been diagnosed with a fatal disease, and must reveal this news to someone dear to them.

43. Write a story using all the following words: *Hospital, Fracture, Mickey Mouse, Sugary, Unlucky*

44. Someone witnesses a murder.

45. Your main character is a parent looking after their child in the park. They get momentarily distracted, and when they look up the child is gone. (Note: If you like, you can write this from the child's point-of-view.)

46. Someone your character loves may be in danger, and your character must reach them before it's too late.

47. Write a story using the following words: *Twin Tower, 9/11, Cellphone, Smoke, Help*

48. Your character has landed the most critical job interview of his or her life, and getting there on time is vital. What happens on the way to jeopardize this journey?

49. The Gestapo raids a home looking for your Jewish character, who is hiding under a bed. While hidden, he or she hears an innocent person being tortured and possibly killed by the officers. Does your character try to come to the rescue, and sacrifice their own life?

50. You main character is a child who has been abused. In this scene, the child has the opportunity to tell the truth to a caring adult who could rescue them, but is too afraid to talk.

51. Write a flash story containing all of the following words: *Headlights, Abandon, Ice, Goodbye, Naked*

52. Pick an exotic location you've never been to and write a vivid scene in which your main

character—a stranger in a strange land—gets hopelessly lost.

53. Your main character is a 20-year-old struggling actor/actress in Los Angeles. Something unexpected happens during an audition.

54. Your cocky character was one of the lead engineers for the World Trade Center, and is certain of the buildings' indomitability. Show the change in his or her psyche as the buildings collapse.

55. A young woman is excited about her new career as a mortician.

56. Write a story using the following terms:
    Adoption, Brazen, Ramshackle, Blue-collar, Blood

57. The politician you loathe most was once a child. Write a scene in which that child is in distress.

58. A person makes a decision to commit a terrible crime. Write a sympathetic scene showing how the character came to that point.

59. Write a flash story containing all of the following words: *Racism, Pink, Fragile, Self-portrait, Hollow*

60. Pick one of your works-in-progress, and rewrite the opening, starting from a later point in the story.

61. Pick a popular TV commercial and rewrite it as a scene from a horror movie or a rom com.

62. Your character knows he or she will lose their eyesight in just a few days. How does she or he spend these last days of sight?

63. Write a story using the following words: *Uptown, Funk, Savage, Patrick Swayze, Bury*

64. Rewrite something you have already written, but with a paranormal or magical realism element.

65. A teacher arrives late at school, only to discover everyone has turned into a zombie.

66. A timid wife is driven to shoot her husband.

67. Write a story using all the following words: *Clone, Apocalypse, Cheeseburger, Blood, Sunlight*

68. A 90-year-old American WWII veteran meets a woman he liberated from a concentration camp over sixty years ago

69. Think about a time in your life that someone hurt you, and write a fictional scene about it ... but write it from the perspective of the other person.

70. Write a story using the following words: *Jack-O-Lantern, Fright, Starlight, Highway, Radical*

71. Pick one of your works-in-progress, and rewrite the opening from a different point-of-view.

72. Two characters are having a meal and talking about the food, only they're not *really* talking about the food.

73. Write a story using the following words: *Vanish, Headache, Love, Buffalo Wings, Autumn*

74. An elderly man is taking a plane ride for the first time in his life. Use precise details.

75. Think about the most negative, pessimistic person you know. Re-imagine them as a

fictional character experiencing astounding good fortune.

76. A recently divorced character gets into a fender bender and discovers the other driver is a long lost love.

77. Your main character is just sitting down to breakfast when the doorbell rings. It's a police officer.

78. Write a dialogue between two characters in which one is keeping a secret from another.

79. Write a story using all the following words: *Ticket, Constellation, Halloween, Starbucks, Sympathy*

80. Your character gets devastating news from a doctor and must tell his or her spouse.

81. With a lot at stake, your main character tries to convince someone to do something illegal.

82. A volunteer at a suicide hotline gets a random call and discovers it's someone they know.

83. Your character has to tell his wife that he wants to have a sex change operation.

84. After a minor car accident, your character exchanges info with the other driver and discovers it's the person from their past they never wanted to see again.

85. Your main character is home watching TV when the doorbell rings. She opens the door and no one is there, but when she looks down, there is a baby in a carrier with a note pinned to its shirt.

86. Write a story using the following words: *Reporter, Seek, Cigarette, Loch Ness, Skeptic*

87. Your character is caught shoplifting. The store owner says that she won't call the police in exchange for a personal favor.

88. A fantasy story that takes place in a futuristic utopian world in which no one ever dies. Then a child's death changes everything.

89. Your character is a writer trying to think of something to write about when the doorbell rings, and standing there is a fictional character (again, choose any character from books, film, etc.). This fictional character wants a role in the writer's story.

90. Your main character is a cop and has just pulled over a female driver for speeding. She seems like a nice old lady, and you are about to let her go with just a warning, when you realize she is your most detested teacher from high school.

91. An angry man who just got bad news discovers a dog has given birth to a litter of puppies on his back porch.

92. A mother reads her daughter's diary and discovers a dark secret.

93. In an ambulance following a terrible car accident, an injured person confesses something to the paramedic.

94. During a job interview, your character notices the boss's fly is unzipped.

95. A battered woman finds the strength to defend herself the only way she can—she kills her husband.

96. A bullied teenager stands up for another kid being bullied.

97. A person gets a chance to choose one superpower for a day.

98. In a fictional authoritarian state, a group of housewives plans an insurrection.

99. An elderly person gets a young racist to see the light.

100. A young person gets an elderly racist to see the light.

SECTION 2
THEMED PROMPTS

These prompts are presented in a format that encourages you to exercise specific writing skills. Each page begins with an explanation of the exercise, followed by five prompts to choose from.

Theme 1: Choose one of the following and write a story with three or more characters …

1. It's Passover Seder and Grandma won't put down her cellphone.

2. Teachers meet about a problem student, but your character thinks they don't understand the kid at all.

3. An elderly parent reveals a shocking secret to his or her adult children.

4. Use all the following terms: *Music, Struggle, Beautifully, Pain Killer, Blame*

5. Rewrite a scene from your work-in-progress, adding more characters.

Theme 2: Choose one of the following and find the moment someone falls in love …

1. A new parents holds their adopted baby for the first time.

2. A first date erupts into an argument … and then everything changes.

3. The marriage has been rocky for years, but as the husband lies bleeding after an accident, the wife holds him in her arms and realizes what love is.

4. Use all the following terms: *Fever, Goosebumps, Swallowed, Casket, Plum*

5. Rewrite a scene from your work-in-progress, inserting a gasp of first love.

Theme 3: Choose one of the following and create a mystery...

1. A woman comes home to find her apartment broken into. The only thing missing: her dog.

2. A man tells his girlfriend to meet him at their favorite restaurant—there's something important he wants to tell her. But he never shows up, and no one knows where he is.

3. After a political rally, all the attendees come down with the same mysterious symptoms.

4. Use all the following terms: *Hotel, Missing, Bedsheet, Spoon, Contagious*

5. Rewrite a scene from your work-in-progress, deepening a mystery.

Theme 4: Choose one of the following and write about a person making a bad choice …

1. A man lies to the police to protect his son.

2. A woman is so furious with her cheating boyfriend she runs over his dog.

3. A teenager shoplifts to impress her friends.

4. Use all the following terms: *Weakness, Friendship, Painful, Giant, Cheated*

5. Rewrite a scene from your work-in-progress, making your character take a wrong turn.

Theme 5: Choose one of the following and write about an animal ...

1. A lost dog winds up in a shelter, and must convince a human not to adopt him, as he knows his owner will come for him.

2. A woman loses her cat and must face her own loneliness.

3. A talking bird.

4. Use all the following terms: *Farm, Sunlight, Pig, Worried, Modest*

5. Rewrite a scene from your work-in-progress, adding a dog.

Theme 6: Choose one of the following and write about a character doing something unexpected …

1. A timid person experiences road rage.

2. A husband admits infidelity to his wife and she reacts.

3. Opening line: This was not the Thanksgiving she expected.

4. Use all the following terms: *Fist, Hurricane, Dizzy, Released, Pearls*

5. Rewrite a scene from your work-in-progress, making a character take a different turn.

Theme 7: Choose any one of the following and write a story that engages the reader in the character's journey …

1. After a brutal capture and horrific crossing, a young African boy arrives in the United States and is sold as a slave.

2. An elderly person wants to move into assisted living, but their adult children are opposed to it.

3. There's a mouse in the bridal suite.

4. Use all the following terms: *Tugged, Ponytail, Squinty, Cattle, Unkind*

5. Rewrite a scene from your work-in-progress, making the character's struggle more vivid.

Theme 8: Choose one of the following and write a romantic or sexy story ...

1. A husband doesn't realize how much he loves his wife until the moment she lay dying in his arms.

2. The date isn't going at all well ... until one of his friends shows up and she feels as if Cupid's arrow has shot right through her heart.

3. A marriage proposal goes awry because she's more interested in sex than what he has to say.

4. Use all the following terms: *Distance, Longing, Heat, Dew, Quarry*

5. Rewrite a scene from your work-in-progress, making it sexier or more romantic.

Theme 9: Choose any one of the following and write a dialogue-heavy scene that does not use the words yes, no, hello or goodbye …

1. Your main character is being followed around by an obnoxious child-ghost no one else can see or hear.

2. A skittish boy pleads with his mother not to smoke a joint before driving him to school.

3. A football player has a panic attack just as the game is about to start.

4. Use all the following terms: *Splashed, Broadway, Curtain, Quiver, Hopeful*

5. Rewrite a scene from your work-in-progress, adding or improving dialogue.

Theme 10: Choose one of the following and write an emotional story in the first person POV or a close third person POV …

1. Think of an argument you had with someone who refused to see your point of view. Write a fictional version of it from the other person's perspective.

2. A fiercely independent elderly person who lives alone is visited by a family member who arrives with brochures, insisting it's time for assisted living.

3. Your character must inform someone a loved one has died.

4. Use all of the following terms: *Betrayal, Silver, Deafening, Airport, Tender*

5. Rewrite a scene from your work-in-progress, digging deeper to reveal an emotional truth.

Theme 11: Choose any one of the following and write a story with a satisfying ending ...

1. Using Romeo and Juliet as inspiration, write a contemporary love story. End it happily or tragically, but make sure the story feels resolved.

2. Write a modern day Cinderella story with an angry protagonist. Give the ending an unexpected twist.

3. Lead with a death, end with a birth.

4. Use all the following terms: *Season, Grudge, Winking, Bridegroom, Fault*

5. Rewrite the ending to one of your pieces, giving it a more satisfying resolution.

Theme 12: Choose any one of the following and write a dialogue-heavy story, making sure the reader knows what the main character is thinking and feeling ....

1. A wife knows her husband is about to confess his infidelity, and doesn't want to hear it.

2. A loving father is at the park with his disabled child when he's confronted by another parent who criticizes him and his child.

3. A woman discovers her business partner has been stealing, and must confront her.

4. Use all the following terms: *Beach, Dusk, Paranoid, White Gold, Burst*

5. Rewrite a scene from your work-in-progress, giving the reader a closer glimpse into the character's emotions.

Theme 13: Choose one of the following and write a scene in present tense ...

1. A window washer witnesses a murder.

2. Use all the following terms: *Disappear, Headache, Love, Laser, Autumn*

3. Everyone in your main character's high school has turned into a Zombie except for this character, his or her best friend, and the one teacher they hate.

4. Your main character is supposed to be babysitting for a younger sibling, who disappears.

5. One of your favorite characters (from book, film, TV, web comics, etc.) finds a kid in trouble and tries to help.

Theme 14: Choose any of the following and write a story in which the setting/environment/ weather plays an integral role ...

1. A honeymoon hike changes the way one spouse feels about the other.

2. A woman attends a big family dinner with news to share: she is terminally ill.

3. An obese person who never leaves the house must finally venture out on the hottest day of the year. What happens when the car breaks down?

4. Use all the following terms: *Rain, Distance, Pocket, Thin Mints, Static*

5. Rewrite a scene from your work-in-progress, giving more weight to the setting.

Theme 15: Choose any one of the following and write a story that involves July Fourth…

1. A refugee experiences Fourth of July fireworks for the first time and has a PTSD episode.

2. Your character feels anything but independent at his/her family's Fourth of July gathering.

3. A child gets lost at a parade.

4. Use all the following terms: *Backyard, Fireworks, Love, Cadillac, Peaches*

5. Rewrite a scene from your work-in-progress, tying it to a holiday.

Theme 16: Choose any one of the following and write a story that ends on a dramatic note …

1. A woman has to tell her boss that another employee has been sexually harassing her.

2. A parent gets called into a meeting with a teacher, expecting the worst.

3. A man cannot reach his elderly father on the phone and panics.

4. Use all the following terms: *Wheelchair, Triumphant, Loophole, Jazz hands, Ensemble*

5. Rewrite a scene from your work-in-progress, ending it on a more dramatic note.

Theme 17: Choose one of the following and write a short piece in which the weather is almost another character ...

1. Changing a tire in the blistering heat.

2. A surprise blizzard on a camping trip.

3. A sudden downpour at an outdoor wedding.

4. A woman who has lived in the tropics her whole life lands in New York in February.

5. Use all the following terms: *Ship, Storm, Prism, Fury, Broken*

Theme 18: Choose one of the following and write a story or scene from the POV of someone very much like yourself ...

1. A friend tells your character he or she hears people who aren't really there.

2. Someone cheats in a race.

3. A minor health issue sends someone into a panic attack.

4. Use all the following terms: *Meltdown, Emergency room, Glass, Sticky, Broken*

5. Your character visits a dying grandparent, who reveals a shocking family secret.

Theme 19: Choose one of the following and write a story or scene from the POV of the opposite sex …

1. A couple is on a long car-ride and one of them has a secret to reveal, but is tortured about it.

2. A teenager tells their parents something they don't want to hear.

3. Use all the following terms: *Shipwreck, Creaked, Watery, Dishonor, Tingle*

4. Your character awakens to discover their last social media post has gone viral … in the worst way possible.

5. Rewrite a scene from your work-in-progress, shifting the point of view to another character.

Theme 20: Choose one of the following and write a story in which one character is a reticent speaker ...

1. A woman who has found evidence of her husband's infidelity confronts him about it, hoping to save the marriage. He has other ideas. (You can reverse the roles here, if you like.)

2. A boss must fire an employee. The catch: they've been having an affair.

3. A person wants to help someone who doesn't want to be helped.

4. Use all the following terms: *Confession, Ugly, Birthday, Souvenir, Taxi*

5. Rewrite a scene from your work-in-progress, making one of your characters secretive.

Theme 21: Choose one of the following and write a story or scene with an opening that grips the reader ...

1. It's the first night of the honeymoon, and it's not going well.

2. Something magical happens to a lonely boy.

3. Someone who's normally shy steps out of their comfort zone.

4. Furious about mistreatment on the job, your character marches into their boss's office to make a formal complaint, only to discover he has been stabbed.

5. Use all of the following words: *Maitre d', Reservation, Critic, Tongue, Anxiety*

Theme 22: Choose one of the following and write a story in which the character's own feelings take him or her by surprise ...

1. Your character wins the lottery.

2. Your character gets the phone call they have been dreaming of for months or years.

3. Your character achieves their dream, i.e., gets a book published, wins an Olympic gold medal, the Tony, Miss America, the Pulitzer Prize, etc.

4. On a morning run, your character discovers a baby bird struggling to survive.

5. Use all the following terms: *Win, Sacrifice, Brittle, Thunderstruck, Joy*

Theme 23: Choose one of the following and write a story in which there is a lot at stake for the main character ...

1. A man is doing the dishes when he hears a strange noise coming from inside his house.

2. Your main character accidentally locks his or her keys in the car.

3. A police officer stops to help a homeless person.

4. Use all the following terms: *Crack, Blast, Emergency Room, Blood, Window*

5. Rewrite the opening of your work-in-progress, raising the stakes for your main character.

Theme 24: Choose one of the following and write a Thanksgiving-themed story ...

1. Your protagonist shows up for Thanksgiving dinner only to discover it's an intervention.

2. At Thanksgiving dinner, one family member knows another's secret, and prods them to reveal it to the rest of the group.

3. Use all of the following terms: *Cornucopia, Grandpa, Betrayed, Football, Apple pie*

4. Your main character dies at Thanksgiving dinner, only to awaken at a table in the afterlife, reunited with loved ones who have passed.

5. A fictionalized version of the Thanksgiving dinner you dread most.

Theme 25: Choose any one of the following and write an action scene …

1. A young wounded war vet, just getting his life back after years of rehab and learning to walk with prosthetic legs, is working as a loan officer at a bank when he hears the unmistakable sound of gunfire.

2. A school lockdown.

3. Your main character is a criminal being pursued by the police.

4. Use all of the following terms: *Stranded, Breathless, Walmart, Crash, Horizon*

5. Someone normally shy and nervous does something heroic.

SECTION 3
ADVANCED THEMED PROMPTS

These prompts are more challenging than those in Section 2, but the format is the same—each page begins with an explanation of the exercise, followed by five prompts to choose from.

Advanced Theme 1: Choose one of the following and dig deep to write about love in the freshest way you can …

1. A gay man has a crush on his co-worker, and he thinks the guy might feel the same way. Only he's not sure if the guy is gay or straight. He makes the terrifying decision to move in for a kiss.

2. A hostile husband turns loving after dementia sets in.

3. A couple meets cute.

4. Use all the following terms: *Flirt, Cocktail, Blue, Wounded, Kiss*

5. Rewrite a scene from your work-in-progress, adding romance.

Advanced Theme 2: Choose one of the following to write a story with a lot of action, or forward momentum ...

1. A couple fights as they make their way through Ikea.

2. A student tries to get to class in a snowstorm.

3. An actual battle.

4. Use all the following terms: Ignition, Caffeine, Arrested, Lucky, German Shepherd

5. Rewrite a scene from your work-in-progress, adding action.

Advanced Theme 3: Write a story in which your characters have an argument that comes to some sort of resolution ...

1. A person with OCD goes into a tailspin when discovering their spouse has rearranged the furniture.

2. An artist's significant other doesn't understand them.

3. Something with time travel.

4. Use all the following terms: *Dressing room, Permission, Bitch, Shattered, Together*

5. Rewrite a scene from your work-in-progress, adding a conflict between two characters.

Advanced Theme 4: Write a story in which your main character has a change of heart ...

1. After a fight with their significant other, your character types out a text apologizing. Before hitting send, she has a change of heart and breaks up instead.

2. A young woman is supposed to sign adoption papers, giving up her parental rights. She is poised, pen in hand, when she flashes back to the brief moment she got to hold and smell her baby.

3. Someone decides not to press charges.

4. Use all the following term: *Asleep, Noise, Whooshing, Risk, Swallowed*

5. Rewrite a scene from your work-in-progress, focusing on the moment your character has a change of heart.

Advanced Theme 5: Choose one of the following and experiment with world-building ...

1. The fascists have won and teachers in the US can be arrested for straying from officially-sanctioned curricula. One teacher struggles to answer an earnest question from a curious student.

2. It's like that Twilight Zone episode, only Henry Bemis's glasses don't break. He just gets really bored with reading.

3. An awards ceremony for Zombie hunters.

4. Use all the following terms: *Sky, Abandoned, Tremble, Citizen, Released*

5. Rewrite a scene from your work-in-progress, conveying your fictional world through subtle cues.

Advanced Theme 6: Experiment with voice. Choose one of the following and write a story in a voice you haven't used before …

1. A young man struggles with seduction as he gets mixed signals from his date.

2. An elderly woman with dementia engages with her hallucinations.

3. A gifted teenager barges into a local politician's office with ideas for improving their city.

4. Use all the following terms: *Canopy, Aisle, Peppered, Silver, Thunder*

5. Rewrite a scene from your work-in-progress, giving it a different tone.

Advanced Theme 7: Write a story with a sympathetic character who behaves badly ...

1. A father steals from a homeless man.

2. A woman takes too much oxycodone and drives her kids to school.

3. A suicide bomber boards a train full of school children.

4. Use all the following terms: *Nametag, Teetotaler, Leering, Beyoncé, Rooftop*

5. Rewrite a scene from your work-in-progress, laying in sympathy for the antagonist.

Advanced Theme 8: Write a story that is more internal than external ...

1. A person is about to knock on their boss's door.

2. A man goes Christmas shopping for his children just days after an accident left his wife in a coma.

3. A person who's broke and hungry sees an old man drop a hundred dollar bill and continue walking, oblivious.

4. Use all the following terms: *Umbrella, Dab, Nurtured, Tortoiseshell, Obedient*

5. Rewrite a scene from your work-in-progress, making it more internal.

Advanced Theme 9: Write a story in which you reveal an altered state of consciousness ...

1. Your stressed-out character attends a party and is given a drink. It's soon apparent there was something in the glass besides alcohol.

2. Your character survives an explosion and wakes up somewhere—possibly a hospital— unable to see or hear.

3. An acid trip.

4. Use all the following terms: *Breathing, Tingle, Stars, Jungle, Drumbeat*

5. Rewrite a scene from your work-in-progress, giving your character an out-of-body experience.

Advanced Theme 10: Write a largely internal story in which two characters meet for the first time …

1. Your world-weary main character is utterly cynical about love—doesn't even believe it exists. Then, in a crowded room, she has a moment straight out of the movies. She locks eyes with a stranger. He's not particularly handsome, but there's something about him that stops the music, drowns out all the other voices. What happens when they finally meet?

2. Create a non-reliable narrator who is so besotted with someone's appearance they overlook a thousand red flags to convince themselves their love object is sublime.

3. A Tinder date.

4. Use all the following terms: *Icy, Arrogant, Handshake, Stevie Wonder, Melt*

5. Rewrite a scene from your work-in-progress, showing us the first meeting between two important characters,

Advanced Theme 11: Do life-altering experiences really change us? Explore this question with one of the following prompts ...

1. Driving to a family dinner, your character already has an attitude. So what if he is an hour late? They can all go to hell if they think they can lay on a guilt trip. Then a road rage incident changes everything, when another driver pulls a gun on your character, taking a shot that misses.

2. Someone thinking of leaving their spouse has a near-death experience.

3. Your wealthy but miserable character discovers she has lost everything in a Madoff-style financial scam.

4. Use all the following terms: *Power Struggle, Barrier, Lottery, Flutter, Kneel*

5. Rewrite a scene from your work-in-progress, exploring the question posed above.

Advanced Theme 12: Choose any one of the following and write a story that takes place in a world very different from our own ...

1. Ten percent of the population is psychic, and they control the government, big business, everything. Show us a scene that sheds light on the oppression of the other ninety percent.

2. It's 1347, and your character is trying to protect his or her family from the Black Plague.

3. Aliens.

4. Use all the following terms: *Icy, Darken, Bone, Shelter, Siren*

5. Rewrite a scene from your work-in-progress, implying facts about the world of your story without being explicit.

Advanced Theme 13: Choose any one of the following and write a story in which the character's feelings are at odds with what he or she is saying ...

1. Your character tries to steal baby formula and is caught.

2. A hiker comes across an injured woman.

3. The bride asks your character why he didn't bring his wife to the wedding.

4. Use all the following terms: *Whisper, Splintered, CPR, Creamy, Static*

5. Rewrite a scene from your work-in-progress, giving your character feelings that contradict the dialogue.

Advanced Theme 14: Choose any one of the following and write a conflict-driven story ...

1. A woman has shunned her father for twenty years, angry that he cheated on her mother. Now the mother is dying and wants the daughter to make peace with the father.

2. A man who's come to peace with his fatal diagnosis wants to refuse chemotherapy, but his wife has other ideas.

3. A scientist is rushing back to the lab to finally see the successful culmination of a lifetime's work, but is pulled over by the police for a broken taillight.

4. Use all the following terms: *Widow, Blunted, Recovery, Damp, Suffocate*

5. Rewrite a scene from your work-in-progress, adding more conflict between characters.

Advanced Theme 15: Choose any one of the following and write a story revealing an emotional truth that feels personal to you. Make the scene fictional, but the emotion biographical ...

1. Think of a time a friend or family member broke your heart. Translate that feeling to a scene with different characters and a different setting.

2. If you've ever been to a funeral that brought you to your knees, recall that feeling. Now create a different character experiencing that same emotion. Give them a backstory different from your own.

3. Think of a moment that made you go white with terror, your reaction so immediate and physical you were nearly overcome. Give that feeling to a character in an entirely different situation.

4. Use all the following terms: *Seep, Fever, Splintered, Cashmere, Money*

5. Rewrite a scene from your work-in-progress, working in an emotional story that feels more authentic.

Advanced Theme 16: Choose any one of the following and write a story that recognizes human sexuality, either with suggestiveness or actual descriptions ...

1. A young couple—it's the first time for both of them. He's more scared than she is.

2. An older couple—neither of whom has slept with anyone for a very long time—end a date in the bedroom.

3. A seduction.

4. Use all of the following terms: *Date, Wine, Shiver, Symphony, Blacker*

5. Rewrite a scene from your work-in-progress, making it sexier.

Advanced Theme 17: Choose one of the following and write a descriptive flash fiction piece ...

1. Your character went blind as an adult, and has resisted trying any new foods since that happened. Write a scene in which this person tries a new food, experiencing it as a blind person.

2. While camping in the woods, an autistic child gets distracted by nature and wanders away from the group he or she is with. Write this from the child's POV.

3. Your character wakes up in a hospital bed unable to hear.

4. Use all the following terms: *Buttery, Iridescent, Gentle, Sticky, Lightning*

5. Rewrite a scene from your work-in-progress, making it more descriptive.

Advanced Theme 18: Choose one of the following and write a piece from deep inside your character's consciousness ...

1. Your character sees a dangerous crime unfolding and must decide whether to intervene.

2. Your character is an ultra-liberal adult with a teenage child. Write a scene in which the teenager comes out as gay, and the parent is surprised by their own reaction.

3. Your character is an ultra-conservative adult with a teenage child. Write a scene in which the teenager comes out as gay, and the parent is surprised by their own reaction.

4. Use all of the following terms: *Nightgown, Floor, Pain, Mary Todd Lincoln, Sunrise*

5. Rewrite a scene from your work-in-progress, making it more internal than external.

Advanced Theme 19: Choose one of the following and write a story in which you take out your frustrations on someone who wronged you …

1.   Create a character based on someone who wounded a person you love. Put them in a situation where they are publicly humiliated.

2.   Think of a situation in which someone asserted their authority over you with cruelty. Write a highly fictionalized version of the event, stripping them of their power.

3.   A family dinner.

4.   Use all the following terms: *Blade, Shiver, Pounding, Feather, Good-bye*

5.   Rewrite a scene from your work-in-progress, working out your personal demons.

Advanced Theme 20: Choose one of the following and write a story in which each character hides a secret …

1. When a college student makes a surprise visit home for the weekend, it should be a joyful reunion. But both the student and the parent are hiding something.

2. A woman brings an injured dog to a vet.

3. A husband can't tell his wife why he won't take the new job he's been offered. The wife won't tell the husband why it's so important for him to accept it.

4. Use all the following terms: *Invitation, Decorations, Melody, Coroner, Soiled*

5. Rewrite a scene from your work-in-progress, giving each character a secret.

Advanced Theme 21: Tap into your lyrical side to find the beauty in something gruesome among these choices...

1. When her spike heel digs into his foot on the dancefloor, it sends a jolt of excruciating pain through him. But he dances on.

2. While chopping meat, she accidentally slices off part of her thumb.

3. She's a superhero who can slow time, and actually watches as his thumb squeezes the trigger and a bullet travels into the victim's flesh.

4. Use all the following terms: *Buttery, Precise, Melting, Cafeteria, Luminous*

5. Rewrite a scene from your work-in-progress, making it more poetic.

Advanced Theme 22: Can people really change? Explore this question with a character who wants to change, needs to change, and is then faced with the moment of truth …

1. His doctor tells him the hard truth: If he stops drinking, he might qualify for a liver transplant. If he keeps drinking, he'll die. He makes up his mind right then he can beat his demons. On the way home, his resolution is put to the test.

2. Your character has a morbid fear of confrontation, but it's time to stop procrastinating and tell her husband the truth. Can she?

3. Since his boyfriend accused him of laughing inappropriately at emotional situations, he's tried to be conscious of this nervous tic. Then his daughter calls with shattering news.

4. Use all the following terms: Sunglasses, Boundary, Jagged, Enamel, Hoped

5. Rewrite a scene from your work-in-progress, focusing on the moment when your protagonist's character is challenged.

Advanced Theme 23: Tapping into the notion that less is more, choose from the following and write an emotional story with restraint ...

1. At a wedding, a father watches as the step-father walks his daughter down the aisle.

2. A veterinarian explains that the dog has to be put down.

3. After a murder trial, your innocent character rises to hear the jury's verdict.

4. Use all the following terms: *Midnight, Awoke, Intruder, Feathered, Weapon*

5. Rewrite a scene from your work-in-progress, making the emotional story bigger by using less words.

Advanced Theme 24: Choose from among the following and write a grounded story with an element of magical realism …

1. A person wrestling with a life-changing decision discovers a portal that allows him to experience the different lives he would have if he made one choice or the other.

2. A woman discovers the fruit tree in her backyard has some magical qualities.

3. An angry child walking in the woods finds a bottle of green liquid. He tosses and breaks it, then discovers a new ability.

4. Use all of these terms: *Watery, Vines, Mystical, Patch, Wounded*

5. Your character is astounded to discover the character in an ancient book is having almost the exact same experiences she is.

Advanced Theme 25: Choose from among the following and humanize someone who seems larger than life.

1.   The president of the United States tries to get his mother to admit she's proud of him.

2.   The world's most famous pop star is in the middle of a performance when she gets a strange cramp and thinks she might be miscarrying.

3.   Oprah gets embarrassed.

4.   Use all the following terms: *Red Carpet, Poisonous, Failure, Hope, Dagger*

5.   Rewrite a scene from your work-in-progress, making a difficult character more human for the reader.

SECTION 4
OPENING LINES

This section lets you choose an opening line to inspire your story. Feel free to change the gender or name of the character, and take the story in any direction.

1. *There were almost too many ice cream flavors to choose from.*

2. *It was a shivery morning, but Deana brought her coffee out onto the porch, a blanket over her shoulders.*

3. *The doctor looked into the distance, as if searching for the right words. Then he pursed his lips, leaned across the desk and gave Isabel the news.*

4. *Adam slipped into the driver's seat and slammed the door.*

5. *With a valid passport and over ten-thousand dollars in the bank, Nina could afford to be reckless.*

6. *They called it a concussion; Leland called it a revelation.*

7. *Chelsea peered through the peephole in the front door, her heart pounding.*

8. *Normally, Lucas wouldn't dream of stealing.*

9. *Bethany stood with her hands at her sides as the man twisted the long balloons into the shape of an elephant.*

10. *Martin was tired of letting his mother push him around.*

11. *It was only a small plate of food—one chicken leg and a tablespoon of peas—but Colette couldn't bear to look at it.*

12. *I tried to move, but my body wouldn't respond.*

13. *Noah jumped overboard without a life jacket.*

14. *Galffogh landed her ship on Zir and opened the pod door.*

15. *On the day Abigail Green decided to kill herself, she ate a simple breakfast.*

16. *Connor climbed the dusty stairs to the attic.*

17. *It was late, and the Vaughan household was shadowy and still.*

18. *Six-year-old Pearl Landers ran into the bathroom where her father was shaving.*

19. *Trembling, Curtis approached the hotel's front desk and cleared his throat.*

20. *I first met Helene in Paris.*

21. *On Fridays, when the final bell rang, the students at Jefferson Elementary stampeded toward the buses.*

22. *The whistling caught her attention,*

23. *Justin's father was blind.*

24. *There were over a hundred employees in the South City Health Clinic, but only five were in the reception area when Kirsten Spier entered with an AK-47,*

25. *Joseph grew tired of explaining why the Mountaintop Inn was located in a valley.*

26. *Paula was embarrassed to admit it.*

27. *"A funeral?" he repeated. "For a cat?"*

28. *Kay glanced down from her balcony and watched the pool boy skim the water for petals and leaves.*

29. *Bruce Morris stayed in his seat, waiting for the people in the aisle of the crowded Airbus to start filing out.*

30. *Vivienne tucked the diary under her bed.*

31. *Peter Gold was about to go into a meeting when the principal of his daughter's school called to say Roxie had bitten one of her classmates.*

32. *The director wanted her naked in the scene.*

33. *Roxie put down the binoculars and turned to her husband.*

34. *It was the fourth straight day of snow, and James needed a plan.*

35. *I pulled out the IBM Selectric I had purchased with my American Express Card and typed out my letter of resignation.*

36. *His father went first, taking a careful step on the rickety basement stairs.*

37. *I wasn't even supposed to be in Ms. Radler's freshman English class.*

38. *It was right there on the Ancestry DNA site: Saul had a half-brother he knew nothing about.*

39. *Violet pushed the stroller into the park, took a seat on the bench, and peered into the carriage of the woman sitting next to her.*

40. *Boot Camp was not what Tom had expected.*

41. *It wasn't your typical stake-out.*

42. *Harriet held onto the fence and watched her brother stare down the pitcher, his well-practiced batting stance close to perfect.*

43. *Less than an hour after my mother's funeral, I could smell weed wafting from my brother's room.*

44. *Camila gave her computer mouse a shake and her screen came to life, revealing an email from her mother's sixth husband.*

45. *It was opening night, and the house was sold out.*

46. *Richard was standing at the stove, watching the edges of a fried egg turn brown, when he decided it was time to leave her.*

47. *Sandra pretended she was sleeping as she listened to the sound of Danny rummaging through her dresser drawers.*

48. *Kenny slipped the tip of his knife into the skin of the bright green pepper and bisected it.*

49. *When An Wang's plane landed in Kennedy Airport, he knew only one person in America.*

50. *He sighed, waiting for an answer, but Kayla still wasn't sure if she wanted to sleep with him.*

51. *Jessica went into the bathroom and saw Zoey's Barbie Doll floating face up in the toilet.*

52. *It started with a pain in his shoulder.*

53. *Compared to the vast waterfront mansion she left behind, Karen's suburban split level was almost quaint.*

54. *He was the most famous artist in Paris.*

55. *Julian folded his arms and sunk into the couch while his mother lectured him on how lucky he was.*

56. *Faith surveyed the room one last time before her book club arrived.*

57. *When she moved in closer and ran a hand up his thigh, Matt knew it would be the kind of afternoon he'd tell his friends about.*

58. *If death wanted to take her, it would damn well wait until she was ready.*

59. *Dustin hated being in love.*

60. *Number Fifty-one Overbrook Drive had a bright red door.*

61. *Allison put on her signal and pulled off the highway, not sure her sputtering Ford would make it to the motel.*

62. *David looked from one end of the casino to the other.*

63. *Eighty years is too long to wait.*

64. *Enrique loved Thanksgiving.*

65. *When I was sixteen, I asked a palm reader how many kids I would have and she took a long pause before answering.*

66. *Once, a Tinder date asked me to tell her the story of my life, and I just laughed.*

67. *"I'm not going in there," the rabbit said.*

68. *On Christmas eve, Ahmed almost missed his flight.*

69. *There was only one person Samantha wanted to call— her sister.*

70. *Jayson Spector kept a careful journal of his time in Iraq.*

71. *There were only three people in front of Lindsey in the return line at Kohl's, but she had already been there twenty minutes and it hadn't moved.*

72. *Max Fielding raised his hand as high as he could, trying to get Ms. Linder to notice him.*

73. *The sky was as gray as dirty dishwater, and Eleanor wished it would rain already.*

74. *Nathan was so engrossed in loading toppings onto his frozen yogurt that he didn't notice his brother glaring at him.*

75. *Wendy looked up, straining to find a constellation she recognized.*

76. *Harlan left everything behind.*

77. *The bungalow was damp and briny.*

78. *When Jo looked at the Caller ID and saw that it was her doctor, she broke into a sweat.*

79. *Ira checked his rifle one last time.*

80. *Jenny reached the kitchen just in time to see her small daughter crack an egg into a sizzling frying pan.*

81. *His mother was killed in one of the nation's most infamous school shootings.*

82. *The receptionist led me to a conference room, where four people sat on one side of the table, waiting to grill me.*

83. *Billy Howell arrived in Los Angeles on a blistering day in August.*

84. *No one made matzo ball soup like my mama.*

85. *Paola's suitcase was almost empty.*

86. *He walked the girl toward the back of the speakeasy and signaled Joe for two drinks.*

87. *Another strange bluish crafts hovered at the end of the field.*

88. *Mae got her children inside just before the twister set down.*

89. *The subway had been hot and sticky, so the first thing Jack did when he arrived home was walk into the bathroom to wash his face, but the sight of a pregnancy test on the counter stopped him cold.*

90. *The email was from her ex-husband's new wife.*

91. *There were only two establishments on Main Street that were still in business.*

92. *Father Garcia lowered his head and crossed himself.*

93. *I hate my name.*

94. *Elsa had a print of Van Gogh's Starry Night hanging over her bed.*

95. *Ray recognized the Caller ID—it was the adoption agency.*

96. *If it weren't for her brother, Olivia would have drowned.*

97. *The pain woke Theo from a black sleep.*

98. *They drove toward the soft, pink dawn.*

99. *Nicki had never been on a cruise before.*

100. *Mrs. Vogel opened her front door to yell at Ben for shoveling her walk.*

SECTION 5
WORD PROMPTS

In this section, each prompt contains five words to use in a story or flash fiction piece. You may change the tense of any verb. Browse through the selections to find one that inspires you, or pick a number from 1-100 and see what you get!

1. *Ache, Fragile, Consent, Paper cup, Burden*
2. *Introduced, Hovering, Devilled egg, Father, Sheepish*
3. *Lost, God, Bubbles, Gritted, Autistic*
4. *Walled, Child, Backpack, Guilt, Necklace*
5. *Cigar, Beverly Hills, Fiery, Bartender, Alibi*
6. *Impulse, Murmur, Diary, Billowy, Token*
7. *Vandalize, Unforgivable, Refrigerator, Persist, Morning*
8. *Martini, Aftershave, Charm, Sister, Testament*
9. *Elevator, Clone, Whistle, Husband, Unlucky*
10. *Hospital, Fracture, Sugary, Mother, Disney World*
11. *Frustrated, Contagious, Fog, Halleluiah, Cologne*
12. *Bitterness, Downtown, Paper bag, Miracle, Candle*
13. *Twin Tower, 9/11, Cellphone, Smoke, Help*
14. *Headlights, Abandon, Ice, Good-bye, Naked*
15. *Adoption, Brazen, Ramshackle, Blue-collar, Blood*
16. *Racism, Pink, Fragile, Self-portrait, Hollow*
17. *Uptown, Funk, Savage, Patrick Swayze, Bury*
18. *Clone, Apocalypse, Cheeseburger, Blood, Sunlight*
19. *Jack-O-Lantern, Fright, Starlight, Highway, Radical*
20. *Vanish, Headache, Love, Buffalo Wings, Autumn*

21. *Ticket, Constellation, Halloween, Starbucks, Sympathy*

22. *Reporter, Seek, Cigarette, Loch Ness, Skeptic*

23. *Music, Struggle, Beautifully, Pain Killer, Blame*

24. *Fever, Goosebumps, Swallowed, Casket, Plum*

25. *Hotel, Missing, Bedsheet, Spoon, Contagious*

26. *Weakness, Friendship, Painful, Giant, Cheated*

27. *Farm, Sunlight, Pig, Worried, Modest*

28. *Fist, Hurricane, Dizzy, Released, Pearls*

29. *Blade, Shiver, Pounding, Feather, Good-bye*

30. *Invitation, Decorations, Melody, Coroner, Soiled*

31. *Tugged, Ponytail, Squinty, Cattle, Unkind*

32. *Distance, Longing, Heat, Dew, Quarry*

33. *Splashed, Broadway, Curtain, Quiver, Hopeful*

34. *Betrayal, Silver, Deafening, Airport, Tender*

35. *Season, Grudge, Winking, Bridegroom, Fault*

36. *Beach, Dusk, Paranoid, White Gold, Burst*

37. *Disappear, Headache, Love, Laser, Autumn*

38. *Rain, Distance, Pocket, Thin Mints, Static*

39. *Backyard, Fireworks, Love, Cadillac, Peaches*

40. *Wheelchair, Triumphant, Loophole, Jazz hands, Ensemble*

41. *Ship, Storm, Prism, Fury, Broken*

42. *Meltdown, Emergency room, Glass, Sticky, Broken*

43. *Shipwreck, Creaked, Watery, Dishonor, Tingle*

44. *Confession, Ugly, Birthday, Souvenir, Taxi*

45. *Maitre d', Reservation, Critic, Tongue, Anxiety*

46. *Win, Sacrifice, Brittle, Thunderstruck, Joy*

47. *Crack, Blast, Emergency Room, Blood, Window*

48. *Cornucopia, Grandpa, Betrayed, Football, Apple pie*

49. *Stranded, Breathless, Walmart, Crash, Horizon*

50. *Flirt, Cocktail, Blue, Wounded, Kiss*

51. *Ignition, Caffeine, Arrested, Lucky, German Shepherd*

52. *Dressing room, Permission, Bitch, Shattered, Together*

53. *Asleep, Noise, Whooshing, Risk, Swallowed*

54. *Sky, Abandoned, Tremble, Citizen, Released*

55. *Canopy, Aisle, Peppered, Silver, Thunder*

56. *Nametag, Teetotaler, Leering, Beyoncé, Rooftop*

57. *Umbrella, Dab, Nurtured, Tortoiseshell, Obedient*

58. *Breathing, Tingle, Stars, Jungle, Drumbeat*

59. *Icy, Arrogant, Handshake, Stevie Wonder, Melt*

60. *Power Struggle, Barrier, Lottery, Flutter, Kneel*

61. *Icy, Darken, Bone, Shelter, Siren*

62. *Whisper, Splintered, CPR, Creamy, Static*

63. *Widow, Blunted, Recovery, Damp, Suffocate*

64. *Seep, Fever, Splintered, Cashmere, Money*

65. *Date, Wine, Shiver, Symphony, Blacker*

66. *Buttery, Iridescent, Gentle, Sticky, Lightning*

67. *Nightgown, Floor, Pain, Mary Todd Lincoln, Sunrise*

68. *Buttery, Precise, Melting, Cafeteria, Luminous*

69. *Sunglasses, Boundary, Jagged, Enamel, Hoped*

70. *Midnight, Awoke, Intruder, Feathered, Weapon*

71. *Watery, Vines, Mystical, Patch, Wounded*

72. *Red carpet, Poisonous, Failure, Hope, Dagger*

73. *Memory, Sore throat, Glass, Salivated, Clumps*

74. *Condemned, Dead-end, Proprietor, Decades, Gazed*

75. *Canvas, Blooming, Chestnut, Enjoyed, Animal*

76. *Whistle, Marigolds, Wept, Newborn, Pale*

77. *Knitting, Mama, Wedgwood Blue, Stumbled, Priceless*

78. *Stamp, Pencil, Bureaucrat, Musty, Untethered*

79. *Opaque, Princess, Sky, Frightened, Melt*

80. *Hidden, Blood, Handgun, Tumbled, Hero*

81. *Silken, Sad, Uncertain, Softening, Ceasing*

82. *Sanctuary, Prayer, Heavenly, Splotch, Devoted*

83. *Terrier, Heartbroken, Sidewalk, Searched, Fat*

84. *Betrothed, Congratulations, Feud, Gasoline, Bells*

85. *Winter, Psychic, Palm, Chilled, Azure*

86. *Brittle, Garden, Dahlia, Trudged, Sunshine*

87. *Classroom, Scissors, Wet, Tiny, Crying*

88. *Balloon, Waved, Elephant, Frozen, Lips*

89. *Naked, Shoulder, Spooned, Accent, Americans*

90. *Bubbles, Alphabet, Teacher, Delayed, Hiding*

91. *Party, Text Message, Alcohol, Wasted, Dead*

92. *Accountant, Doctor, Lawyer, Wedding, Shattered*

93. *Spirit, Motes, Connected, Blackest, Message*

94. *Gleaming, Stainless Steel, Birdcage, Freedom, Pop*

95. *Rumbling, Weather, Stomach, Complained, Queasy*

96. *Alone, Frightened, Crisp, Buzz, Investigate*

97. *Orchard, Bees, Scent, Picked, Fallen*

98. *Enclosed, Check, Empty, Ink, Bleeding*

99. *Poodle Skirt, Ponytail, Rink, Fluffy, Laughed*

100. *Pennies, Vegetarian, Thankful, Devoured, End*

SPARKS

ABOUT THE AUTHOR

Ellen Meister is a published author, creative writing instructor and coach, editor, ghostwriter, and public speaker. Her books include:

Devil in the Details (Mira Books, January 2020)
Dorothy Parker Drank Here (Putnam, 2015)
Farewell, Dorothy Parker (Putnam 2013)
The Other Life (Putnam 2011)
The Smart One (HarperCollins 2008)
Secret Confessions of the Applewood PTA (HarperCollins 2006)

For more information or to sign up for her mailing list, visit ellenmeister.com.

Made in the USA
Middletown, DE
30 November 2021